26 CHILDREN'S S·O·N·G·S

ARRANGED BY DENES AGAY

Interior illustrations by Janice Fried

ISBN 978-1-5400-8336-4

Visit Hal Leonard Online at
www.halleonard.com

Contact us:
Hal Leonard
7777 West Bluemound Road
Milwaukee, WI 53213
Email: info@halleonard.com

In Europe, contact:
Hal Leonard Europe Limited
42 Wigmore Street
Marylebone, London, W1U 2RN
Email: info@halleonardeurope.com

In Australia, contact:
Hal Leonard Australia Pty. Ltd.
4 Lentara Court
Cheltenham, Victoria, 3192 Australia
Email: info@halleonard.com.au

Alouette

Traditional
Arranged by Denes Agay

Moderately

mp A - lou - et - te, gen - tille a - lou - et - te, A - lou - et - te,

je te plu - me - rai. Je te plu - me - rai la tête, je te plu - me - rai la tête;

f Et la tête! et la tête! A - lou -ette! A - lou -ette! Oh, A - lou - et - te,

gen - tille a - lou - et - te, A - lou - et - te, je te plu - me - rai.

Animal Fair

American Folksong
Arranged by Denes Agay

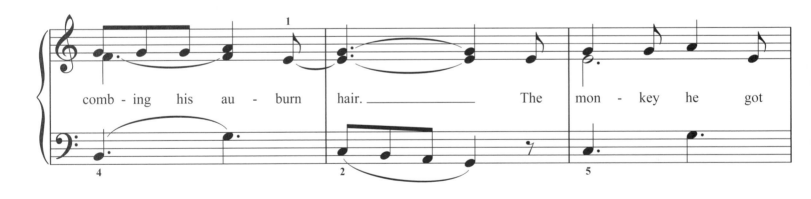

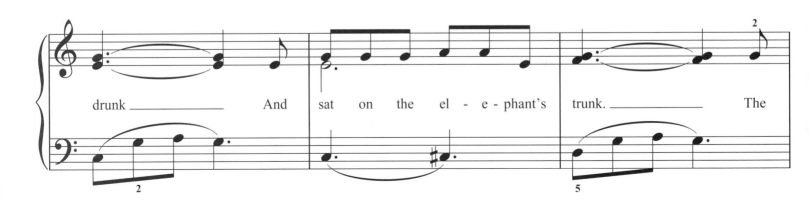

Baa, Baa, Black Sheep

Traditional
Arranged by Denes Agay

Moderately

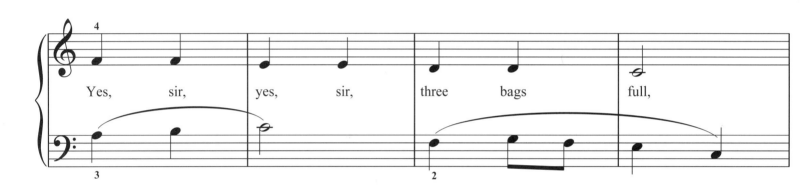

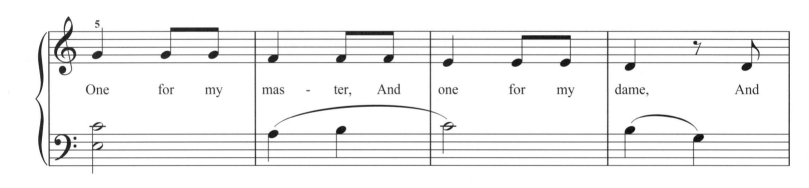

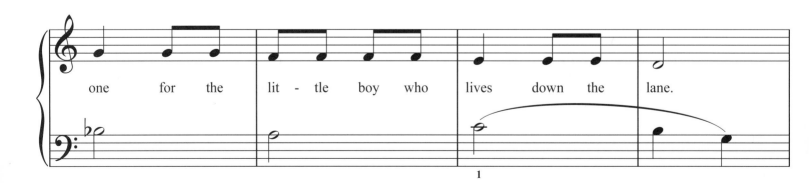

Baa, baa,. black sheep, have you an-y wool?

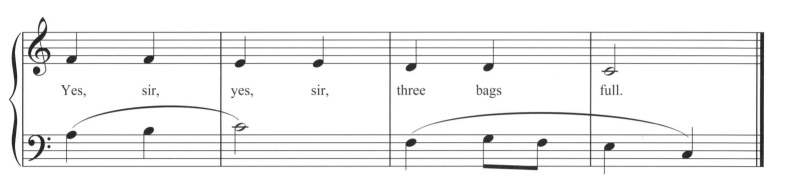

Yes, sir, yes, sir, three bags full.

The Bear Went Over the Mountain

Traditional
Arranged by Denes Agay

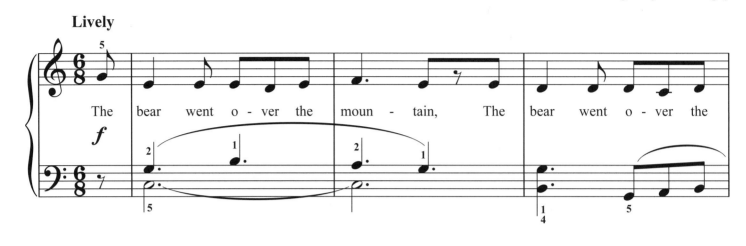

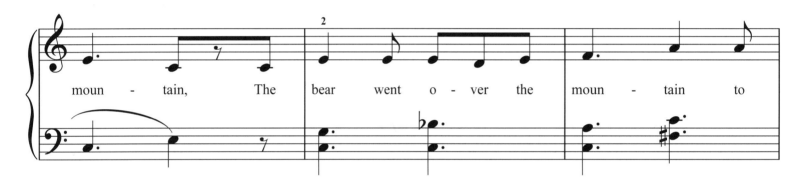

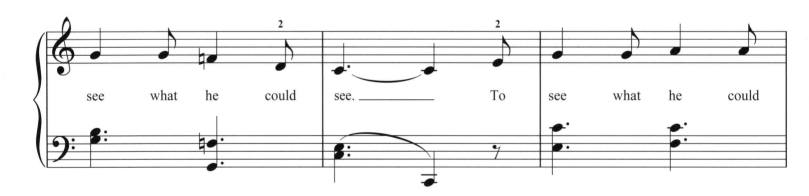

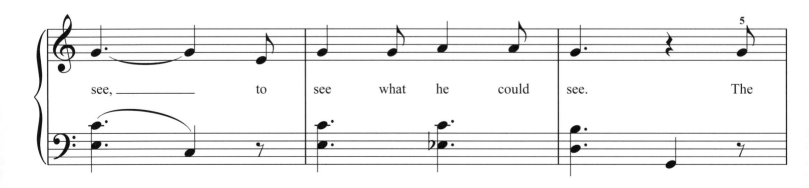

bear went o - ver the mountain, the bear went o - ver the mountain, the

bear went o - ver the moun - tain to see what he could see._____

Chiapanecas

Mexican Folk Song
Arranged by Denes Agay

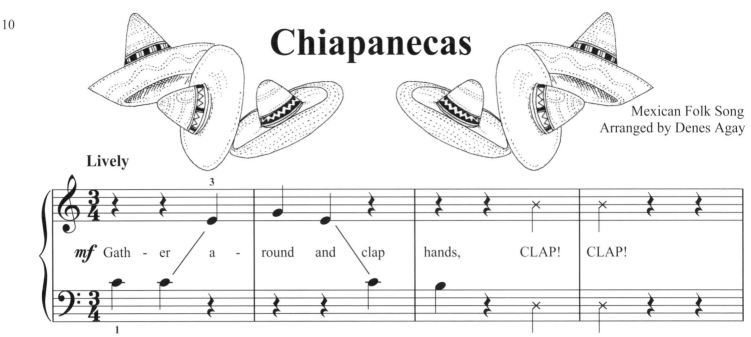

Lively

Gath - er a - round and clap hands, CLAP! CLAP!

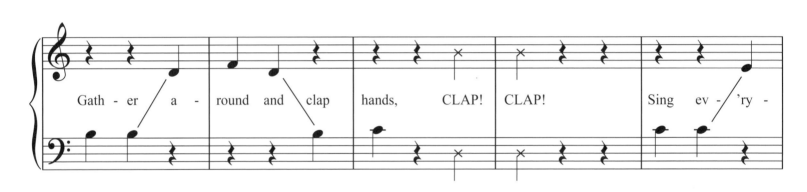

Gath - er a - round and clap hands, CLAP! CLAP! Sing ev - 'ry -

one and clap hands, CLAP! CLAP! Join in the fun and clap

hands, CLAP! CLAP! Ay, ay, Dance ev - 'ry -

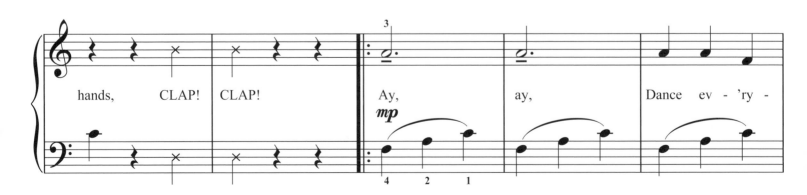

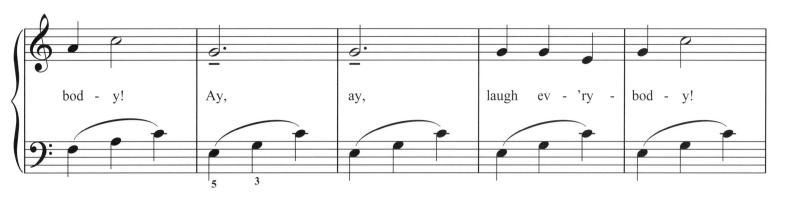

bod - y!   Ay,   ay,   laugh ev - 'ry - bod - y!

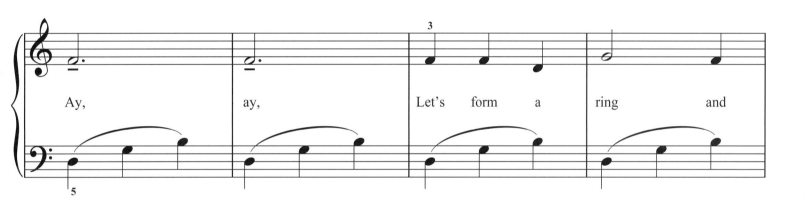

Ay,   ay,   Let's form a   ring   and

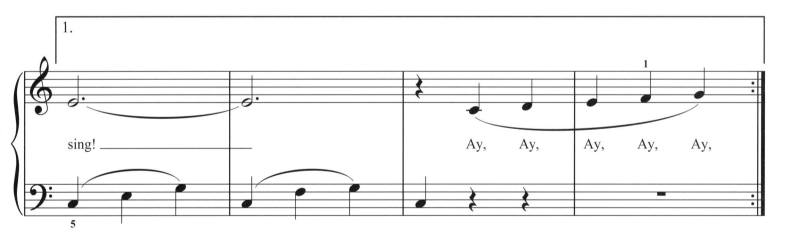

sing! _____   Ay, Ay,   Ay, Ay, Ay,

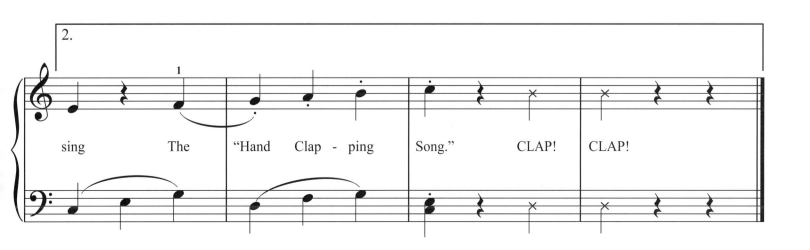

sing The   "Hand Clap - ping   Song."   CLAP!   CLAP!

Bingo

Traditional
Arranged by Denes Agay

The Farmer in the Dell

Traditional
Arranged by Denes Agay

Are You Sleeping?

(Frère Jacques)

Traditional
Arranged by Denes Agay

Here We Go 'Round the Mulberry Bush

Traditional
Arranged by Denes Agay

If You're Happy and You Know It

Words and Music by L. Smith
Arranged by Denes Agay

Very perky

If you're hap - py and you know it, clap your hands, CLAP! CLAP! If you're

hap - py and you know it, clap your hands, CLAP! CLAP! If you're

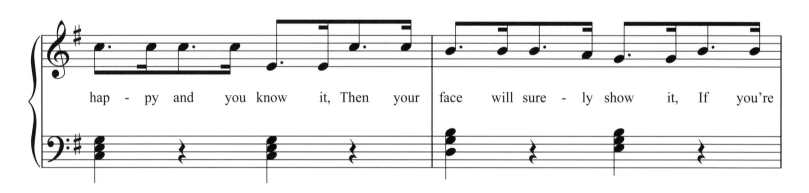

hap - py and you know it, Then your face will sure - ly show it, If you're

hap - py and you know it, clap your hands. CLAP! CLAP!

Itsy-Bitsy Spider

Traditional
Arranged by Denes Agay

Jack and Jill

Traditional
Arranged by Denes Agay

Kookaburra

Words and Music by Stan Wakefield
Arranged by Denes Agay

Koo - ka - bur - ra sits in the old gum tree. ___

Mer - ry, mer - ry king of the bush is he. ___ Laugh, Koo - ka - bur - ra

laugh, Koo - ka - bur - ra, gay your life must be.

London Bridge Is Falling Down

Traditional
Arranged by Denes Agay

Lon - don Bridge is / fall - ing down, / Fall - ing down, / fall - ing down.

Lon - don Bridge is / fall - ing down, / My fair / la - dy.

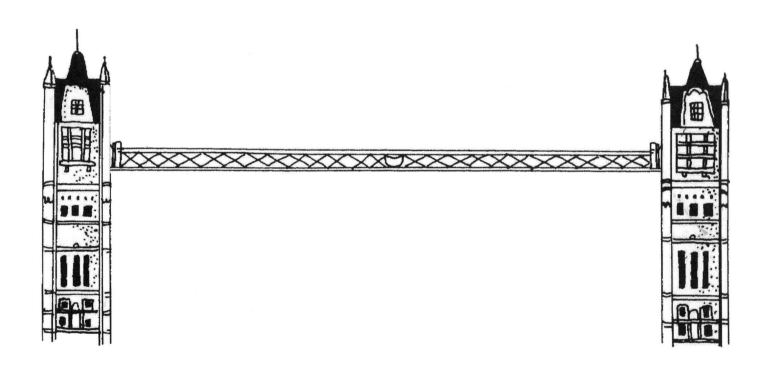

Mary Had a Little Lamb

Words by Sarah Josepha Hale
Traditional Music
Arranged by Denes Agay

The More We Get Together

German Folk Song
Arranged by Denes Agay

Oh Where, Oh Where
Has My Little Dog Gone?

Words by Sep. Winner
Traditional Melody
Arranged by Denes Agay

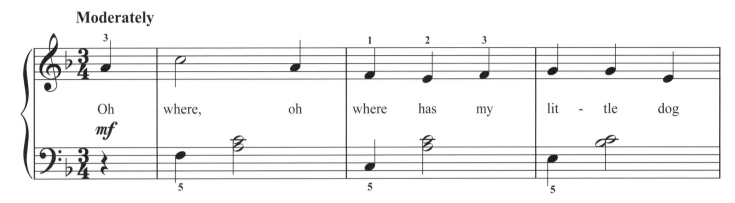

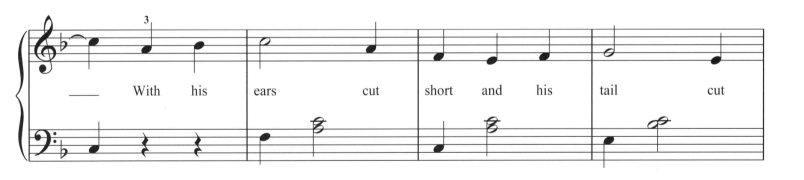

Old MacDonald

Traditional
Arranged by Denes Agay

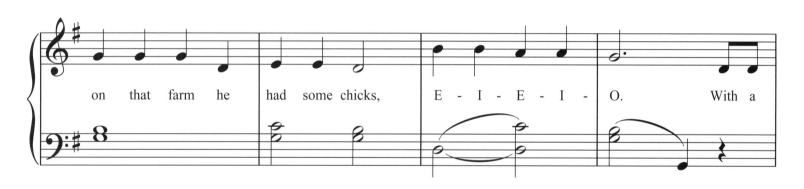

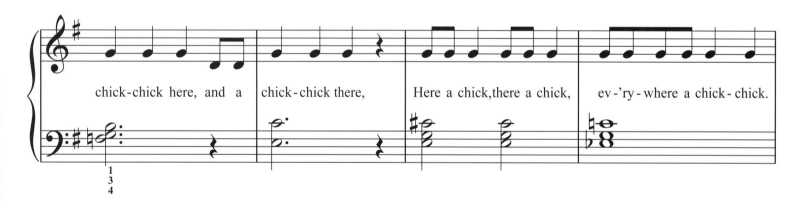

Pop! Goes the Weasel

Traditional
Arranged by Denes Agay

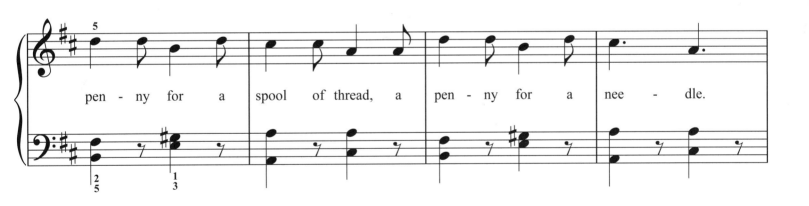

Rock-a-bye Baby

Traditional
Arranged by Denes Agay

Gently swaying

Optional Ending

Row, Row, Row Your Boat

Traditional
Arranged by Denes Agay

Sing a Song of Sixpence

Traditional
Arranged by Denes Agay

Merrily

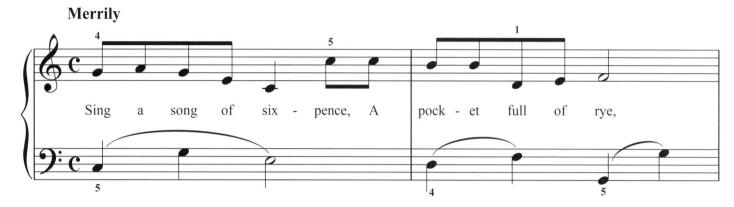

Sing a song of six - pence, A pock - et full of rye,

Four and twen - ty black - birds   Baked in a pie.   When the pie was o - pened, The

birds be - gan to sing;   was - n't that a dain - ty dish to   set be - fore the king?

This Old Man

Traditional
Arranged by Denes Agay

Merry walking tempo

mf This old man, he played one, He played nick - nack on my drum,

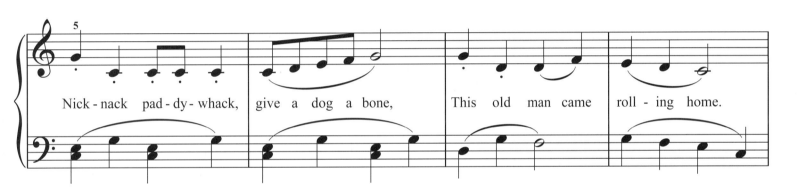

Nick - nack pad - dy - whack, give a dog a bone, This old man came roll - ing home.

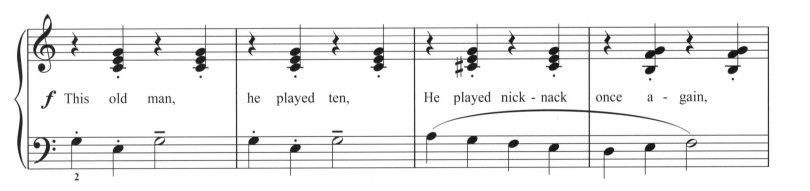

f This old man, he played ten, He played nick - nack once a - gain,

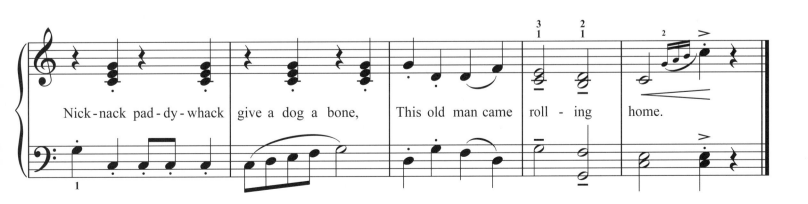

Nick - nack pad - dy - whack give a dog a bone, This old man came roll - ing home.

Three Blind Mice

Traditional
Arranged by Denes Agay

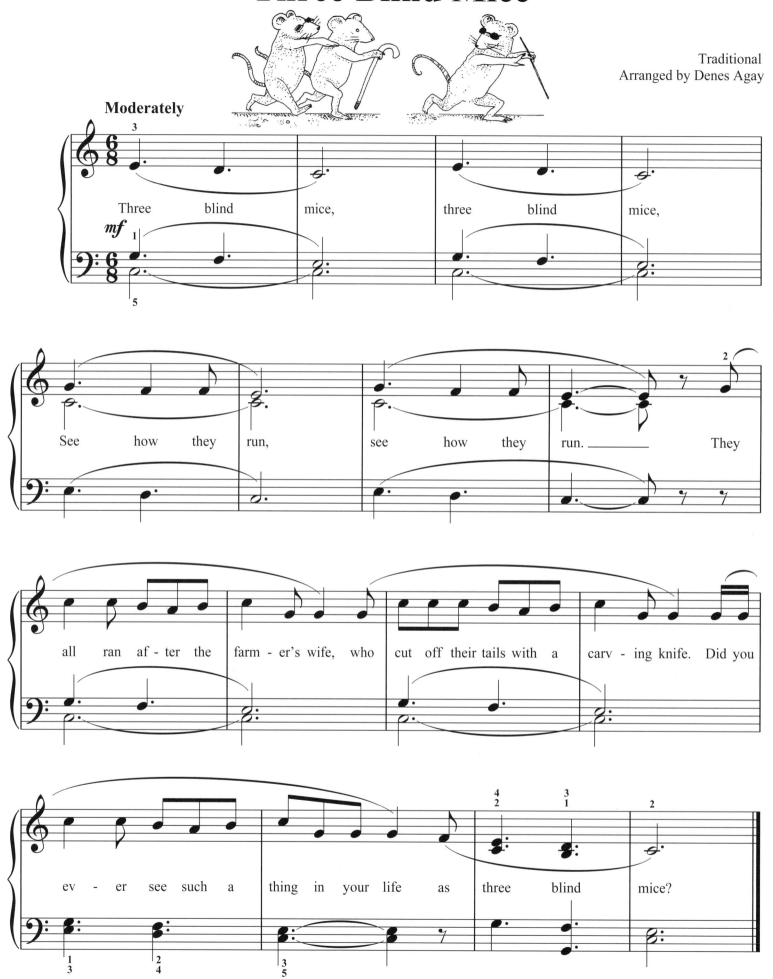

Moderately

Three blind mice, three blind mice,

See how they run, see how they run. _____ They

all ran af - ter the farm - er's wife, who cut off their tails with a carv - ing knife. Did you

ev - er see such a thing in your life as three blind mice?

The Wheels on the Bus

Traditional
Arranged by Denes Agay

Yankee Doodle

Traditional
Arranged by Denes Agay